30 Model Essays
Q1-30

LIKE TEST PREP

CONTENTS

Write a Test Essay in 25 Min.

1. Time yourself with a countdown watch or a stopwatch. When you cannot finish within the given time limit, mark it. Give yourself enough time to finish your essay. Practice writing essays this way.

2. Outline before you write an essay. Write an essay only when you have a good outline. A good outline contains a persuasive argument, compelling supports, and three or more historical/literary examples. Ask your writing tutor to give you comments on the appropriateness of the examples or quotes in your outlines and essays.

3. Get your essays scored and corrected on the use of vocabulary, grammar, punctuation, and organization by a writing tutor. Ask him/her to score your essay each time you submit a revision. Revise until you get a score above 8 out of 12 total. If you feel like you need a higher standard, set 10 out of 12 for a passing paper.

4. Practice rewriting the revised essay until you know how to write it blindfolded. Practice writing it within 22-23 minutes. Then, give yourself 2-3 minutes to review what you wrote before you submit it. Once you have one great essay, you can apply your knowledge (vocabulary, expressions, and examples, and arguments) and skills (essay organization skills and the ability to write a quality essay within the given time) in writing other essays.

5. Practice rephrasing the sentences from your reading and model essays. Circle the words or expressions you would like to learn. Create new sentences with them. You can look up the dictionary or ask your writing tutor to help you with them.

6. There are a lot of similar topics on essay tests. Get a list of commonly appearing essay topics and categorize the most common ones together so that you can apply the same logic and examples on similar essay topics.

7. Practice outlining in your mind with the common test essay topics. You may take notes as you think of arguments and examples.

1. Argument

2. Support 1: 1-2 examples

3. Support 1: 1-2 examples

4. Support 1: 1-2 examples or Counter-argument: examples

5. Concluding Statement

If you can come up with a good outline in five or six sentences in 3-5 minutes, consider yourself quite successful.

HOW TO WRITE A TEST ESSAY
-THE APPEARANCE

Your Test essay should look like a four or five paragraph essay with a clear introduction, body and a conclusion. We suggest four or five paragraphs because you need to provide more than two examples and one body paragraph is not enough for that. In terms of length, make sure you fill out both pages given to you.

Your essay represents you. Write in good handwriting and try not make a mess on your paper. If your essay is neat and orderly, that's what you are to them as the essay graders don't know your name, gender, age, or the school you attend. They only see you on paper. They can only make assumptions.

Also remember that your essay is scored holistically, meaning that the essay graders scores your essay based on its overall impression. They have a score in mind as they read it. They are trained to give an essay a 4 or a 5. You want to give your essay graders a favorable impression, right?

Introduction
Body 1-support 1
Body 2-support 2
Body 3-support 3or Counter-argument
Conclusion

Introduction
Body 1-compare/contrast or advantages/disadvantages
Body 2- compare/contrast or advantages/disadvantages
Conclusion

HOW TO WRITE A TEST ESSAY -THE OVERALL STRUCTURE

Paragraph one is the introduction. You may start your essay with a famous/relevant quote to the topic that only educated people know and can recognize that you are smart, although your readers don't know everybody and every literature on the planet. Do not ramble on with pointless some people say this and others say that. Focus on presenting a clear and thoughtful argument backed up by strong supports. Don't be wishy-washy and swing like a pendulum. You can enumerate them (e.g. first, second, third). Your introduction should be a guide through your essay.

Start the second paragraph with a topic sentence. and then provide specific examples from history, literature, and current events. Provide dates and names of incidents and people. Be accurate. You can end your second paragraph or give a preview your third paragraph.

Start the third paragraph with a topic sentence. and then provide specific examples from history, literature, and current events. Provide dates and names of incidents and people. Be accurate. You can end your third paragraph or give a preview your fourth paragraph.

Start the fourth paragraph with a topic sentence. and then provide specific examples from history, literature, and current events. Provide dates and names of incidents and people. Be accurate.

In your conclusion, you can summarize what you said in your essay and make a conclusion. If the content and the logic of your body paragraphs were rich and convincing, you would find it easy writing this part. Don't be too specific like you were in the body paragraphs as it is time to end your argument. Be general. You may end with a quote if you want but try not to abuse them.

HOW TO WRITE A TEST ESSAY -ADVANCED WRITING SCORING RUBRIC

This table shows you what you need in your essay for a high score. Try to avoid the problems on the left side: stay on the right. You will do well.

Length	no conclusion	Less Than 1 Page	1 Page	1 & 1/2 Page	2 Pages
Language	Poor	Fair Spoken Slang Cliché	Average Simple	Good Flowery Redundant	Excellent Abstraction Academic & Neutral
Grammar	Poor	Fair	Average	Good	Excellent
Spelling & Punctuation	Poor	Fair	Average	Good	Excellent
Organization	Poor	Fair	Average Formulaic	Good	Excellent
Examples	Irrelevant	Relevant but not specific	Hypothetical	Personal	Historical Current Literary
Creativity	Poor	Fair	Average Formulaic	Good	Excellent
Argument	Poor Absolute Claim Irrelevant	Fair	Average	Good	Excellent counter-argument
Content	Off-Topic Poor	Poor	Fair	Average	Excellent
Clarity	Poor	Fair	Average	Good	Excellent
Persuasiveness	Poor	Fair	Average	Good	Excellent
Handwriting	Poor	Fair	Average	Good	Excellent

HOW TO WRITE A TEST ESSAY
-THE OUTLINE

1. argument

2~3. at least 2 supports 1-2 examples each

4. argument+why

1. Argument:: We can benefit from learning about the flaws of famous figures.

2. Support 1: We can learn from the achievements of famous people, and nobody is perfect ex) Achilles, Hercules, Odysseus, Hector, Alexander the Great, Princess Diana, JFK all had personal flaws.

3. Support 2: We don't make the same mistakes as the famous people did. ex) We don't have to live miserable lives like Sylvia Plath/Virginia Wolf.

4. Counter-argument: However, not all famous people's flaws are acceptable or valuable. ex) H. Truman using the atomic bomb in Hiroshima on civilians to stop WWII is unacceptable just like Hitler and Churchill cannot be excused from the blame of attacking the innocent civilians.

5. Thesis: Important lessons can be learned from the flaws of famous people without risking our lives or precious resources. (argument+why).

HOW TO WRITE A TEST ESSAY
-THE INTRODUCTION

There are myriad ways to write an essay, but here I suggest two. Try to imitate these until you develop your own style. Sample 1 ends with a thoughtful argument, and Sample 2 ends with a preview of the body. Try not to go too specific and try not to use examples in the introduction.

Sample 1

Intro-The discovery that someone we admire has done something wrong is always disappointing and disillusioning. Yet even when people we consider heroes have been tarnished by their faults, they are no less valuable than people who appear perfect. <u>When we learn that an admired person, even one who is seemingly perfect, has behaved in less than admirable ways, we discover a complex truth: great ideas and great deeds come from imperfect people like ourselves.</u>

Sample 2

Intro-Changing decisions when circumstances change is often better than sticking to the original plan. Living in human society, people are often expected to stick to their original plans to be consistent. <u>However, one needs to be flexible in order to wisely adapt to fast changing situations.</u> Examples can be given in the cases of Ralph Waldo Emerson, Bertrand Russell, and Vladimir Lenin.

Body-Emerson in his _____ essay argued that one does not need to be consistent.

HOW TO WRITE A TEST ESSAY
-THE BODY

1. Try to use as many abstractions and nominalizations (big words) as possible. Try to hit the nail at once with that one word instead of beating around the bushes.
(an equal opportunity policy that allows a certain percentage of colored students to be admitted to schools that serves public: <u>affirmative action</u>) (sentencing someone to death: <u>capital punishment</u>) (right to vote: <u>suffrage</u>) (protesting without violent behavior: <u>non-violent passive resistance</u>) (human beings are free from destiny or God's plans: <u>free will</u>) (depending on each other: <u>interdependence</u>)

2. Avoid overused expressions. Substitute simple words with difficult one.
(many->plethora) (attend->matriculate) (cry->lament) (cause->induce) (ignore->disdain) (to do list->agenda) (change->enhance or redirect) (honorable->dignified) (instead of->as an alternative to) (end->pull out of) (think of->devise)

3. Use nominalizations instead of simple verbs.
(prefer->preference) (disturb->deter->deterrence)

4. Use educated expressions, examples, and quotations from few famous people that is applicable in many different situations and practice using them.
 (Descartes' "<u>cogito ergo sum</u>": I think, therefore I exist) (<u>a priori</u>: before) (<u>magnum opus</u>: a masterpiece) (<u>mens rea</u>: guilty mind) (<u>albeit</u>: in spite of) (<u>tabula rasa</u>: an empty table)

5. Try to connect your body paragraphs. Build good transitions so that your ideas flow from one to another more smoothly (See Sample 2 on page v.)

Here, two body paragraphs are given as an example. The author starts with a clear topic sentence (one of the most...) at the beginning of the body paragraph. The specific names mentioned (World War I, Fritz Haber, "father of chemical warfare," Media Awareness Network (2010)) gives power and authority to the essay.

Also note that the transition (In addition...) between body paragraphs is smooth as the second paragraph can use the first paragraph as a support to further discuss the topic. <u>Use proper quotations or at least make your essay sound like you are quoting an important person or media.</u>

Sample Body

<u>One of the most detrimental effects of technology is how it makes war more violent and destructive</u>. For example, one of the reasons why <u>World War I</u> was one of the deadliest conflicts of all time is because we were able to manufacture many fatal weapons by utilizing improved technology. During this war, combatants expanded the use of catastrophic armaments, such as machine guns, combat planes and tanks. These deadly machines were made possible by <u>the application of scientific knowledge</u> developed by scientists, including a Dutch chemist, <u>Fritz Haber.</u> He used his knowledge to introduce chlorine gas, earning him the "father of chemical warfare" title.

<u>In addition</u>, violence can be generated by exposure to diverse media, such as television and the internet, which are also products of technology. <u>Media Awareness Network (2010) argues that</u> naive young people can be harmed by identifying themselves with brutality displayed in the media. This demonstrates that technology not only affects the global village, but may also increase aggression in people.

HOW TO WRITE A TEST ESSAY
-THE CONCLUSION

Rephrase and summarize in your conclusion. You can reopen your conclusion with a general statement. Then summarize your specific points that you discussed in the body paragraphs. Make a concluding statement which incorporates your statements. Do not discuss anything specifically or suggest examples in this section. <u>Do not talk about any arguments, supports, or examples that you did not mention in the body paragraphs.</u> Be concise and stay focused.

Sample Conclusion

While we enjoy the convenience and advancements made possible by the development of technology, we must not overlook the side effects of the process. In order to assure our future existence and to prevent cataclysmal events, governments around the globe must devise plans to cope with problems facing mankind. <u>Perhaps the most crucial task humankind has to implement is to ex-cogitate an eclectic solution that will allow us to reap the benefits of technology, while not being overwhelmed by its negative aspects.</u>

1. Are actions more important to consider than people's intentions?

It is very important to try to understand people's moti vations before judging their actions. Egregious, outrageous behavior may appear to stem from innate evilness but ther e are factors in play that are not perceptible to outsiders. A person may appear harmful and inconsiderate but perhaps the person was confronted with extraneous circumstances. People should always try to understand why people act the way they do.

Understanding other people is far more important tha n indicting people through a moral framework. The foundi ng of psychology as a discipline came after that of religion and is an evolutionary offshoot of many moral philosophie s. Instead of judging people through black and white moral notions, evil and good, bad and good, the primary focus of psychology is to understand the inner workings of the min d.

Nietzsche, in his *Genealogy of Morality*, claimed that the re is no fixed moral universe, and that morality itself is subj ect to change according to culture. With the discipline of p sychology and some moral philosophies in mind, it can be said that the nature of a strange individual cannot be encap sulated with narrow words such as inconsiderate, harmful, and evil.

Moving away from the sciences and philosophy, there are factors in play that are not observable by outside partie s. For example, a village may consider a local boy as absolu tely contemptible because he steals bread from bakers, and puts on his back stolen clothes hung on a clothesline by ne ighbors. But upon closer inspection, this very child may co me from a broken home with little supervision from his gu ardians who failed to teach him basic ethics. Indeed with t he case of this neighborhood thief, a moral indictment is le ss prudent than attempting to understand the upbringing o f the child.

Moreover, there is a sense of permanence when pron ouncing a certain moral or personal attribute onto others. People change, and therefore personality descriptors shoul d hardly be used to judge others. A sentence of judgment i s a finality to the object being judged. However harmful, in considerate, outrageous personality traits will more than lik ely undergo change. Inconsideration of others may have be en a psychological reaction to being taken advantage of by friends and acquaintances. As soon as this outlook on peo ple is adjusted, so does the inconsideration to people. Ther efore, pronouncing a fixed judgment on a person is far fro m dependable.

In conclusion, it is best not to judge people according to hindsight evaluations of their actions. There are many fa ctors leading people to act the way they do. Moreover beca use people change, and pronouncing judgment is a sort of final opinion to the issue, it is best to rely on science and p sychology when making personality assumptions.

Model Sentences of Essay # 1

1. Egregious, outrageous behavior may appear to stem fro m innate evilness but there are factors in play that are not perceptible to outsiders.

2. A person may appear harmful and inconsiderate but per haps the person was confronted with extraneous circumsta nces.

3. The founding of psychology as a discipline came after th at of religion and is an evolutionary offshoot of many mor al philosophies.

4. Nietzsche, in his Genealogy of Morality, claimed that th ere is no fixed moral universe, and that morality itself is su bject to change according to culture.

5. With the discipline of psychology and some moral philo sophies in mind, it can be said that the nature of a strange i ndividual cannot be encapsulated with narrow words such as inconsiderate, harmful, and evil.

6. For example, a village may consider a local boy as absolu tely contemptible because he steals bread from bakers, and puts on his back stolen clothes hung on a clothesline by ne ighbors.

7. People change, and therefore personality descriptors sho uld hardly be used to judge others.

8. Moreover because people change, and pronouncing judgment is a sort of final opinion to the issue, it is best to rely on science and psychology when making personality assumptions.

2. Which is better for society: when its members simply follow the ideas of leaders or when its members act as individuals?

A society with limited restrictions on the expression o f ideas and opinions is better off than a society with a prop ensity to censor. A society does not reach its full potential socially, culturally, and economically when members of soc iety are threatened for being truthful.

Evidence shows that healthy democracies have within their nation-state boundaries a vibrant press and media. In contrast, societies that are steeped in paranoia, which are ty pically operated from under a tyrannical state and by a dict atorship, are bankrupt from the sort of mechanisms that le ad people to openly share their opinions on art, politics, lif estyle choices, and mutual interests commonly seen among societies with a free and open press.

A society with people who incessantly copy the ideas and opinions of others are typically under external pressure to do so, and as a result of such insipid social imitation, the rate of social, economic, and cultural development that wo uld otherwise transpire in a free and open society is weak. A society composed of men and women who are not boun d by popular convention is a society - when coupled with p ositive economic factors – with the most amount of happi ness.

There is a measurable improvement in overall social h appiness when certain members of any given society is allo wed to express their unique ideas. Since all societies, open or not open, have conventions on what is appropriate and not appropriate, what is true and not true, it is still importa nt that societies allow outlier members to deviate from con vention.

As soon as the deviation from medium social behavio r is not allowed, there is a measurable decline in overall soc ial happiness, as there are certain members who are being c ensored and affected unfavorably. Moreover, the historical pattern has shown that free and open societies develop at a faster and healthier rate. A society is structurally unsound when members of society copy the ideas and opinions of o thers.

When George Orwell released 1984, the threat of co mmunism was a very real threat to the West. The book pai nted a picture of a society with limited freedom to express. As a result, this Orwellian society suffered in its productio n of the arts, literature, and economic development. Expre ssionism was so stifled that the press officer of the republi c, Senior Mellenieuv, went unchallenged as he mandated th e discontinuation of the color purple from the spectrum of colors. Indeed, in this Orwellian society, the fact that mem bers of society copied the idea that the color purple does n ot exist, signified that the society was structurally unsound due to the authoritarian government.

It is not necessary to cite Orwellian, dystopian societi es when there are modern-day examples. Contemporary na tion-states with a long track record of human rights violati ons often stifle the freedom to express ideas and opinions. Take, for example, the current crisis in Syria: President Bas har is carrying out a violent crackdown on protesters who are merely expressing their opinion on the current govern ment of their country.

Although being natural born citizens, these protesters are not allowed to express their opinions. As a result, there are fierce conflicts transpiring in Syria. Contemporary Syria is a case where lack of individuality and freedom to express has enraged a segment of the population, causing internal s trife, and economic depression. The society of Syria is stru cturally unsound as long as there are individuals who must copy the ideas and opinions of others in order to remain sa fe.

In conclusion, society is better off when individuals ar e allowed to interact and express without persecution. As s oon as fear is used to pressure individuals to contain indivi dualism, society as a whole stumbles developmentally. A fr ee and open society has the highest amount of happiness, a nd such prosperity is reflected by its economic, cultural, an d political development.

Model Sentences of Essay # 2

1. A society with limited restrictions on the expression of ideas and opinions is better off than a society with a propensity to censor.

2. Evidence shows that healthy democracies have within their nation-state boundaries a vibrant press and media.

3. In contrast, societies that are steeped in paranoia, which are typically operated from under a tyrannical state and by a dictatorship, are bankrupt from the sort of mechanisms that lead people to openly share their opinions on art, politics, lifestyle choices, and mutual interests commonly seen among societies with a free and open press.

4. Since all societies, open or not open, have conventions on what is appropriate and not appropriate, what is true and not true, it is still important that societies allow outlier members to deviate from convention.

5. Contemporary nation-states with a long track record of human rights violations often stifle the freedom to express ideas and opinions.

6. A society composed of men and women who are not bound by popular convention is a society - when coupled with positive economic factors – with the most amount of happiness.

7. Contemporary Syria is a case where lack of individuality and freedom to express has enraged a segment of the population, causing internal strife, and economic depression.

8. As soon as fear is used to pressure individuals to contain individualism, society as a whole stumbles developmentally.

9. A free and open society has the highest amount of happiness, and such prosperity is reflected by its economic, cultural, and political development.

10. The society of Syria is structurally unsound as long as there are individuals who must copy the ideas and opinions of others in order to remain safe.

3. Are mainstream views and ideas more likely to be valid?

The truth and facts have little to no correlation to what is popular or mainstream. Although human nature seeks the truth, it is also succumbs to dubious information for a variety of reasons. There are instances in which false information gives comfort to people or provides physical safety from provocateurs, making them forego basic logic.

Since people have only the observation of natural phenomena and the scientific method and, finally, each other to validate their claims, it is often the case that the nodding of heads is sufficient for false information to become the conventional idea. As history shows, widely held views often have a shelf life, being popular for affected generations until a watershed event or scientific breakthrough causes people to question widely held beliefs and dogma.

Prescribed doctrine proclaimed as unquestionably true by a particular group is a sort of religious dogma. Conversely, when challenging the unquestionable, there are consequences, especially in societies where certain widespread tenets are held dangerously sacred. In the case of ideas where views are not to be challenged, many people, although na turally predisposed to seek the truth, will tap into their first instinct to survive and therefore revert to what is safe to say. Here safety is more important than communicating the truth. There is ample evidence in history to suggest that fear and persecution compel people to accept the unreasonable as fact.

The inquisition in Early-Modern Spain is a striking example on how fear of persecution compelled many to abstain from science and philosophy. Although many early-modern European artists and writers traced their birth to the Iberian Peninsula, Northern Europeans associated the region with "the black legend." The black legend finds its most usual expression, that is, its typical form, in judgments about cruelty, superstition, and political tyranny. Aside from the construed cruelty and political tyranny of the Spanish government towards native peoples in the Americas, catholic dogma and superstition rampant among the Spanish population caused many Northern Europeans to believe the peninsula opposed the spiritual progress and intellectual activity of the North.

Catholic Europe is an example on how religious dogma, being the widespread belief among the population, lagged the population behind the North in scientific achievem ents and human rights. For example, when the Italian astronomer, Galileo, defended the tenets of Heliocentricism, believing that the Sun was the center of the solar system not the Earth, the Catholic administration in Italy persecuted him. Christian scripture at the time was taken literally.

In the instance of Galileo's trial, the biblical reference, Psalm 104:5, which says "the Lord set the earth on its foundations; it can never be moved" was cited as evidence against what would become a commonly known fact, that the Earth is indeed not the center of the universe. The persecution of Galileo by the widespread belief that the Earth was indeed the center of the universe is a striking example in history on how common held beliefs are not always correct.

In conclusion, the truth and facts often do not reflect what is popular. People nod their heads to common beliefs for a variety of reasons. Many times, people believe in widely held beliefs in order to remain safe, despite whether the beliefs are commonsensical.

Model Sentences of Essay # 3

1. The truth and facts have little to no correlation with what is popular or mainstream.

2. Although human nature seeks the truth, it is also succumbs to dubious information for a variety of reasons.

3. There are instances in which false information gives comfort to people or provides physical safety from provocateurs, making them forego basic logic.

4. Since people have only the observation of natural phenomena and the scientific method and, finally, each other to validate their claims, it is often the case that the nodding of heads is sufficient for false information to become the conventional idea.

5. As history shows, widely held views often have a shelf life, being popular for affected generations until a watershed event or scientific breakthrough causes people to question widely held beliefs and dogma.

6. Conversely, when challenging the unquestionable, there are consequences, especially in societies where certain widespread tenets are held dangerously sacred.

7. In the case of ideas where views are not to be challenged, many people, although naturally predisposed to seek the truth, will tap into their first instinct to survive and therefore revert to what is safe to say.

8. The inquisition in Early-Modern Spain is a striking example on how fear of persecution compelled many to abstain from science and philosophy.

9. Catholic Europe is an example on how religious dogma, being the widespread belief among the population, lagged the population behind the North in scientific achievements and human rights.

10. The persecution of Galileo by the widespread belief that the Earth was indeed the center of the universe is a striking example in history on how common held beliefs are not always correct.

4. Is it better for people to be realistic or optimistic?

I think being realistic is better than being headlessly optimistic. It is more advantageous to understand the facts and obstacles of any given action or goal taken than being optimistic and thereby headstrong and dreamy. Although it can be said that realistic people lack long term goals and are short sighted, the reverse can be said about optimistic people. The latter group does not have the proper perspective to achieve short term goals in order to eventually reach their lofty, long term goals. Realistic people have in their mental arsenal the ability to get short term goals completed, allowing them to, inch by inch, reach loftier goals mirroring the optimists.

One reason why being a realist is better than being an optimist, is because facts and the situation at hand is far more important than simply wishing a desirable outcome. Realists are closely related to pragmatists. William James, the father of Pragmatism, espoused the practical approach to problems and affairs. Pragmatists are more concerned with how to get from A to B, and then from B to C, and so forth, than are the optimists. Hypothetically, optimists may desire greatly to reach destination C, but have no sense of pragmatism to conquer A and B first.

Furthermore optimists are too headstrong. It is a sig n of measurable intelligence when a laboratory animal thro wn into a skinner's box, being tested on positive and negati ve stimuli, stops electrocution by repeating the same action . In a sense the dreamy optimist is similar to a non-sentient laboratory animal, clicking repeatedly on a button without knowing what will transpire immediately thereafter. The re alist, being a cousin of the pragmatist, is most concerned w ith the immediate consequence of an action.

In conclusion, there are many advantages to being rea listic, and many disadvantages to being optimistic. Realists understand the facts and obstacles and therefore often ma ke informed decisions. On the other hand, optimists are to o headstrong and dreamy and therefore make many mistak es, and continue to make them without veering from their course.

Model Sentences of Essay # 4

1. Although it can be said that realistic people lack long term goals and are short sighted, the reverse can be said about optimistic people.

2. The latter group does not have the proper perspective to achieve short-term goals in order to eventually reach their lofty, long term goals.

3. Realistic people have in their mental arsenal the ability to get short term goals completed, allowing them to, inch by inch, reach loftier goals mirroring the optimists.

4. In a sense the dreamy optimist is similar to a non-sentient laboratory animal, clicking repeatedly on a button without knowing what will transpire immediately afterwards.

5. The realist, being a cousin of the pragmatist, is most concerned with the immediate consequence of an action.

6. On the other hand, optimists are too headstrong and dreamy and therefore make many mistakes, and continue to make them without veering from their course.

7. Realists understand the facts and obstacles and therefore often make informed decisions.

Optimists are too headstrong and dreamy and therefore make many mistakes, and continue to make them without veering from their course.

> 5. Should government employ everything at its
>   disposal to protect citizens?

The function and the role of the government has bee n debated upon for ages without any concrete answer bein g offered as to how much is exactly enough or even too m uch. Especially with today's so-called declaration of "War on Terror," we have witnessed a pre-emptive war, aggressi on inflicted in the name of national security as an unavoida ble misfortune practiced by a government in order to prote ct its citizens.

Although such political situations are far from being s imple, what seems clear is the necessity for a type of utilita rian perspective that is neither totalitarian nor xenophobic. A government shall never exercise absolute power no matt er what the point of justification may be, for the possibility of ill consequence is too great.

The reason why fear is perhaps the supreme apparatu s of political propaganda is that fear naturally induces the n eed for security, and thus, it could be utilized as a powerful agent for governmental control. Limitations on freedom a nd individual rights deceptively come as an inevitable sacrif ice that is first said to apply only to the accused or the "oth er." As citizens first do not believe that the tightened grip applies to them personally, they are willing to forgo their civil liberties for that heightened sense of security. However, what they do not realize at that moment is that once the legal device is put into place, the classification of inclusivity remains flexible.

We have witnessed this to be true countless times. The fact that wartime sacrifices civil liberties simply illustrates this. In the time of war, logic, reason, and compassion, all characteristics usually heralded as the epitome of humanity often fail to apply. Consequently, in the time of insecurity, the prime role of government becomes the protection of its citizens through any means necessary, which by definition transcends any "boundary" in the legal sense of the term.

George Washington, one of the founding fathers, as a matter of fact, the first President of the United States, keenly warned us of the delicate role of the government for "government is not reason; it is not eloquent; it is force. Like fire, it is a dangerous servant and a fearful master." And thus, like fire, it should always be kept on a close watch and a careful distance, for if the heat of the patriotic flame were to ever get too extreme, the almost invisible haze of smoke will blind our sight from recognizing even our own sister.

Model Sentences of Essay # 5

1. The function and the role of the government has been d ebated upon for ages without any concrete answer being of fered as to how much is exactly enough or even too much.

2. Especially with today's so-called declaration of "War on Terror," we have witnessed a pre-emptive war, aggression i nflicted in the name of national security as an unavoidable misfortune practiced by a government in order to protect i ts citizens.

3. Although such political situations are far from being sim ple, what seems clear is the necessity for a type of utilitaria n perspective that is neither totalitarian nor xenophobic.

4. The reason why fear is perhaps the supreme apparatus o f political propaganda is that fear naturally induces the nee d for security, and thus, it could be utilized as a powerful a gent for governmental control.

5. Limitations on freedom and individual rights deceptivel y come as an inevitable sacrifice that is first said to apply o nly to the accused or the "other."

6. As citizens first do not believe that the tightened grip ap plies to them personally, they are willing to forgo their civil liberties for that heightened sense of security.

7. However, what they do not realize at that moment is tha t once the legal device is put into place, the classification of inclusivity remains flexible.

6. Are some dreams worth the ultimate price – death?

Dreams can go beyond a career choice and material desires. They can relate to belief systems. Of course, dreams are worth dying for if they have been examined closely and are based on a foundation of justice and righteousness.

Today, for example, South Korean armed forces face a situation that tests their commitment to democracy and freedom - and that could lead to their untimely deaths. So, the lives and dreams of South Korean military forces, along with the citizens they are defending, are on the line.

Indeed, tensions remain high on the Korean peninsula after the recent North Korean artillery attack on South Korea's Yeonpyeong Island that left four South Koreans dead and nearly 20 injured. And some top South Korean officials, including Won Sei-hoon, the chief of the National Intelligence Service, believe that North Korea will likely attack again.

With the possibility of war on the horizon, South Korean forces must again ask themselves whether they are willing to die for democracy and freedom. Such deliberations must go beyond mere nationalism and defending one's cou ntry. Human rights are at issue. North Korea has a totalitarian form of government that subjugates the human rights and well-being of its people. Friedrich Durrenmatt, the late Swiss novelist, told us what's necessary to protect human rights: "Only the freedom of mind can prevent the state from becoming totalitarian and from issuing totalitarian demands."

At the risk of being overly sentimental, it remains profound to say freedom is a human right and should be protected with death if necessary. So, yes, dreams are worth dying for if they have been analyzed and understood. South Korea's military service members and citizens are in harm's way. And, they have dreams indelibly tied to freedom. Those dreams may soon come face to face with, and be tested by, the North Koreans.

Model Sentences of Essay # 6

1. Dreams can go beyond a career choice and material desires.

2. Dreams are worth dying for if they have been examined closely and are based on a foundation of justice and righteousness.

3. South Korean armed forces face a situation that tests their commitment to democracy and freedom - and that could lead to their untimely deaths.

4. With the possibility of war on the horizon, South Korean forces must again ask themselves whether they are willing to die for their democracy and freedom.

5. Such deliberations must go beyond mere nationalism and defending one's country.

6. North Korea has a totalitarian form of government that subjugates the human rights and well-being of its people.

7. At the risk of being overly sentimental, it remains profound to say freedom is a human right and should be protected with death if necessary.

8. Indeed, tensions remain high on the Korean peninsula after the recent North Korean artillery attack on South Korea's Yeonpyeong Island that left four South Koreans dead and nearly 20 injured.

> 7. Should education emphasize creativity as much as literacy and mathematics?

These days, the purpose of education these days seems to be a straightforward one: to equip the student with the tools to be a financial success. Making money and gaining status are the twin goals of our materialistic society. Of course, being a success socially and financially is a worthy thing; we all have to eat, and we would all like to enjoy the benefits of prosperity. However, the soul craves self-expression more than money, and schools should and must promote creativity.

To begin with, the world is currently suffering the effects of a money-above-all culture. Financial institutions around the globe have collapsed as a result of the blind pursuit of profit by money managers, stockbrokers, and banks. The Bible says, "The love of money is the root of all evil." Money is good, but meaning is better. Making our way in the world, finding what we were meant to do and what brings us happiness, is what leads to a happy life. Happy people make others happy, too, and one painting or poem can tell us more about the meaning of life than a thousand spreadsheets.

The famous American psychologist Abraham Maslow found that, once certain basic needs (such as food, shelter, and safety) are met, the amount of income someone has is no predictor of happiness. Millionaires are as likely to be m iserable as 40-hour-a-week office workers. Rather, the high est goal of humans is self-actualization. That is, people nee d to express their hopes, fears, dreams, and talents. School s need to encourage dance, poetry, sculpture, and as many methods of self-expression as they can, in order to produc e happy, productive, creative graduates ready to share their gifts to the world.

Our school systems need to encourage students to us e every form of thought they're capable of producing. Sir Ken says, "We think about the world in all the ways that w e experience it. We think visually, we think in sound, we th ink kinesthetically, we think in abstract terms, we think in movement." Only by using all of their talents can people b ecome all they are meant to be. Those who have the most t alent in the fields favored by traditional education, such as science and mathematics, will still rise to the top.

In the final analysis, traditional education has brought the world to the state it's in today. If we want an overcrow ded, overheated world in conflict, we should keep doing w hat we have been doing in our schools. However, if we wa nt a sane, humane, creative world full of possibilities, we n eed to follow Sir Ken's advice and encourage our children' s talents. They will blossom like flowers and fill the world with their colors.

Model Sentences of Essay # 7

1. Financial institutions around the globe have collapsed as a result of the blind pursuit of profit by money managers, stockbrokers, and banks.

2. The famous American psychologist Abraham Maslow found that, once certain basic needs (such as food, shelter, and safety) are met, the amount of income someone has is no predictor of happiness.

3. Millionaires are as likely to be miserable as 40-hour-a-week office workers.

4. Schools need to encourage dance, poetry, sculpture, and as many methods of self-expression as they can, in order to produce happy, productive, creative graduates ready to share their gifts to the world.

5. Our school systems need to encourage students to use every form of thought they're capable of producing.

6. However, if we want a sane, humane, creative world full of possibilities, we need to follow Sir Ken's advice and encourage our children's talents.

7. They will blossom like flowers and fill the world with their colors.

8. Is happiness the result of one's decision to be content in life?

The greater part of our happiness or misery indeed depends on our dispositions and not our circumstances. It may be in fact that our circumstances themselves may be determined by our state of mind, so better emotions lead to improved circumstances.

First, we must acknowledge that there are certainly circumstances that cannot be altered simply by happy thoughts. An individual on a sinking ship needs to find a lifeboat, and this reality will not be changed by positive thinking. However, this may of course be considered an emergency situation, not something that people face on a daily basis. For the person in more mundane circumstances, a positive attitude will go a long ways towards consistent happiness.

Secondly, we have examples from history as evidence. The trials of Job eventually led to the restoration of his family and wealth to a degree he had never seen before. One man, over the course of 28 years lost his job, failed twice in business, failed several times to win elections, and had a nervous breakdown. In 1860, Abraham Lincoln was elected president of the United States. Thomas Edison is well k nown for failing primary school, resorting to home schooli ng by his mother, but he is even more famous for the inve ntions that these successes became.

It's difficult to gauge whether these successes equate t o happiness or misery, there is unfortunately no shortage o f miserable successful men. Some of these arguably success ful individuals were indeed content and happy with their lif e, but others were not happy and in fact, they were misera ble and depressed. Their success could not curtail the happ iness or lack of happiness produced by their disposition.

A friend of motivational and business speaker Robert J Ringer bears this out. His friend retired, and began maki ng stained glass lamps as a way to pass the time. After doi ng this for several months, he found himself on the beach one day, and a feeling of utter contentment washed over hi m. Sadly it lasted only a short period. With the success in making, and then selling his lamps, he found himself hiring employees, dealing with accounting, and back in the same r at race he had retired from. His friend briefly found solace and happiness, and then, in pursuing more income by ope ning a business, the entrepreneur no longer felt satisfied wi th life.

Finally, it is obvious that emotions such as happiness

are to a large part under our control. A person has the ability to take a set of circumstances into consideration and choose his emotional response for better or for worse. Martha Washington speaks the truth when she says that happiness or misery is dependent on our disposition, and not or circumstances.

Model Sentences of Essay # 8

1. The greater part of our happiness or misery depends on our dispositions and not our circumstances.

2. An individual on a sinking ship needs to find a lifeboat, and positive thinking will not change this reality.

3. Thomas Edison is well known for failing primary school, resorting to home schooling by his mother, but he is even more famous for the inventions that these successes became.

4. It's difficult to gauge whether these successes equate to happiness or misery, there is unfortunately no shortage of miserable successful men.

5. Some of these arguably successful individuals were indeed content and happy with their life, but others were not happy and in fact, they were miserable and depressed.

6. With the success in making, and then selling his lamps, he found himself hiring employees, dealing with accounting, and back in the same rat race he had retired from.

7. His friend briefly found solace and happiness, and then, in pursuing more income by opening a business, the entrepreneur no longer felt satisfied with life.

8. Finally, it is obvious that emotions such as happiness are to a large part under our control.

> 9. Which is more important to the international community: the nation-state or the individual?

Between the nation-state and the individual, the nation-state is the most important symbol to the international community. Although there are international monitoring agencies with the sole objective of overseeing human rights issues, the rights of people are second to the geopolitical situation of nations. Put in another way, the nation-state dominates the spotlight while individuals receive disproportionately less attention. The distribution of power within the United Nations will be analyzed to decipher whether the nation-state as a political entity receives more attention than individuals.

The organization that measures the international pulse is the United Nations. Created immediately after the Second World War, the organization is a collaboration of global nations sharing common interests such as global stability and peace. Individuals representing their nations are ranked and ordered by the country of which they represent. Despite being called the United Nations, the organization is not egalitarian in its distribution of power and representative voting power. The United Nations does not allocate equita ble powers to Nations according to their global share of th e human population, but instead the paradigm of power wi thin the organization is based on economic, historical, and military factors.

Although there are One hundred and ninety-six count ries, only five nations dominate the United Nations. Only t he United States, Russia, China, France, and England have veto powers that can overturn the majority opinion of othe r nations. Aside from China and the United States, the sec urity council has a relatively low population count compare d to nations such as India, Indonesia, Brazil, and even Nig eria. If individuals were a more important symbol to the in ternational community, then countries with a larger amoun t of people would naturally command more authority in th e United Nations.

The historical, economic, and military situation of de mographically large nations following the Second World W ar, are the reasons for their lack of power in the United Na tions. The economic order in 1945 was firmly concentrate d in the West, with the exception of Japan. The economic power of nations closely related to their military capacity, a s advanced weaponry and ability to mobilize hundreds of t housands of soldiers required a strong industrial base. Wit h a massive population dwarfing the European powers co mbined, the sub-continent and ancient civilization of India did not become a Security Council member because of its weak industrial economy and colonial tributary status. The economic and military power of nations was not the only f actor in the years following World War II.

With the case of Japan, a telling prerequisite for dema nding more power in the United Nations was the political situation of nations. Defeated nations aligned with Nazi G ermany were automatically denied entrance, leaving Italy, J apan, and West and East Germany, great economic and mi litary powers, out of the running. Indeed, the structure of t he United Nations, the great symbol of International coop eration, was designed by a group of militarily battered nati ons after World War II.

In conclusion, it is more likely that nation-states recei ve more attention from the media and powerful organizati ons than do individuals. The symbol of international conse nsus and pulse, the United Nations, awards more power an d authority to nations based on their economic, military, an d historical circumstances than their demographic situation . If individuals were more important and symbolic to the in ternational community than nation-states, then nations wit h larger populations would command a proportionate amount of power in the United Nations.

<u>Model Sentences of Essay # 9</u>

1. Although there are international monitoring agencies with the sole objective of overseeing human rights issues, the rights of people are second to the geopolitical situation of nations.

2. The distribution of power within the United Nations will be analyzed to decipher whether the nation-state as a political entity receives more attention than individuals.

3. Created immediately after the Second World War, the organization is a collaboration of global nations sharing common interests such as global stability and peace.

4. Individuals representing their nations are ranked and ordered by the country of which they represent.

5. Aside from China and the United States, the security council has a relatively low population count compared to nations such as India, Indonesia, Brazil, and even Nigeria.

6. If individuals were a more important symbol to the international community, then countries with a larger amount of people would naturally command more authority in the United Nations.

7. The economic power of nations closely related to their military capacity, as advanced weaponry and ability to mobilize hundreds of thousands of soldiers required a strong industrial base.

8. With a massive population dwarfing the European powers combined, the sub-continent and ancient

civilization of India did not become a Security Council member because of its weak industrial economy and colonial tributary status.

9. The symbol of international consensus and pulse, the United Nations, awards more power and authority to nations based on their economic, military, and historical circumstances than their demographic situation.

10. Only the United States, Russia, China, France, and England have veto powers that can overturn the majority opinion of other nation.

10. Is apathy just as harmful to humans as causing physical pain?

I disagree that apathy is just as harmful to humans as causing physical pain. Unjust and unwarranted anger and hatred is much more damaging to the human soul than apathy. The apathetic man may be persuaded to take up the challenge if given solid reasons for doing so. Indifference, however, is not an end, but merely a stage in the intellectual process.

As an example, take the inhumane events of the Holocaust in the 1940's. Americans were indifferent to the plight of the Jews throughout most of the war, hearing stories of persecution, but, since they had been subjected to dubious propaganda during the First World War, they were much more skeptical of anti-German propaganda during the early years of the second one.

The plight of the Jews was unknown until the liberation of the Kaufering camp in 1945. Indifference was washed away by righteous anger that led directly to the prosecution and in some cases execution of those responsible through the Nuremberg trials.

What led to the persecution of the Jews in the first pl

ace? Hatred, inculcated and long developed hatred and anger. I would say additionally that what held the Germans from doing anything while their brothers and sisters were subjected to their torments was not indifference but cowardice.

I do believe there is a causative relationship between indifference and the mass effect of genocide. The indifference of the German public to the Jewish plight under the Nazi regime was as detrimental as explicit support. Despite Nazi Germany being a single state totalitarian government, there was no significant domestic resistance against their governmental policies. Instead the German public was generally supportive of their government.

To sum up, although apathy to violence and prejudice does not prevent mass suffering, it is hardly the most significant factor to it. The major factor leading to suffering akin to the Holocaust is pure hatred against a minority group such as the German Jews.

Model Sentences of Essay # 10

1. Unjust and unwarranted anger and hatred is much more damaging to the human soul than indifference.

2. Unjust and unwarranted anger and hatred is much more damaging to the human soul than apathy.

3. The apathetic man may be persuaded to take up the

challenge if given solid reasons for doing so.

4. Indifference, however, is not an end, but merely a stage in the intellectual process.

5. As an example, take the inhumane events of the Holocaust in the 1940's.

6. Americans were indifferent to the plight of the Jews throughout most of the war, hearing stories of persecution.

7. Since they had been subjected to dubious propaganda during the First World War, they were much more skeptical of anti-German propaganda.

8. The plight of the Jews was unknown until the liberation of the Kaufering camp in 1945.

9. Indifference was washed away by righteous anger that led directly to the prosecution and in some cases execution of those responsible through the Nuremberg trials.

10. What led to the persecution of the Jews in the first place?

11. Hatred, inculcated and long developed hatred and anger.

12. What held the Germans from doing anything while their brothers and sisters were subjected to their torments was not indifference but cowardice.

13. I do believe there is a causative relationship between indifference and the mass effect of genocide.

14. The indifference of the German public to the Jewish plight under the Nazi regime was as detrimental as explicit

support.

15. Despite Nazi Germany being a single state totalitarian government, there was no significant domestic resistance against their governmental policies.

16. Instead the German public was generally supportive of their government.

17. Although apathy to violence and prejudice does not prevent mass suffering, it is hardly the most significant factor to it.

18. The major factor leading to suffering akin to the Holocaust is pure hatred against a minority group such as the German Jews.

11. Is striving to achieve a goal always the best course of action, or should people give up if they are not making progress?

Imagine a world without the light bulb, without civil r ights, or without the personal computer. If the forerunners of all of these concepts and inventions had given up at the first sign of failure then we would be living in a very differ ent world today. Striving to achieve a goal is always the bes t course of action, even if it may seem like one is not maki ng progress. Edison failed thousands of times before he fi nally progressed beyond failure and invented a working lig ht bulb. Martin Luther King Jr. kept the fight for civil right s in America going, despite slow to no progress in the dese gregation of America. Bill Gates stood stuck in the same pl ace for years until finally moving forward to invent the per sonal computer.

Thomas Edison is known today as a great inventor, b ut this was not always the case. He was also known as the man who just couldn't get it right, when it came to certain i nventions. He made no progress for years in the area of ele ctricity and if had given up, who is to know how long we would have lived with oil lanterns and candlelight lamps. D

espite failing again, and again, Edison forged ahead, becom
ing one of the most important inventors in history. The lig
ht bulb hasn't changed much from what Edison designed y
ears ago, but it was only possible because he worked towar
d achieving his goals.

Progress in the desegregation movement in America
was slow moving if not completely sedentary during the ti
me of the great Rev. Martin Luther King Jr. Despite great
opposition from the majority white population in the Sout
h and government officials, King moved forward striving t
owards the equality he so desperately want for himself and
the other African Americans in the United States. His tena
city inspired others to join the fight, creating a movement.
It all culminated into his moving "I have a dream speech"
which is still used to inspire people around the world. If M
artin Luther has given up at the first sign of no progress, w
e might be living in a very different America. Instead we ha
ve an African-American President and separate and equal i
s no longer an accepted practice.

Bill Gates dropped out of school, only to become one
of the richest men in America. It took him several years to
develop the PC and Windows operating system. He has sin
gle handily changed the face of communication in today's s

ociety. Had he stopped at the first sign on difficulty, we mi ght not have the technology we have today.

Progress doesn't always come quickly, and sometimes i t doesn't come at all. What separates ordinary people from extraordinary people and their ground breaking inventions and influence, is tenacity. From Thomas Edison to Rev. M artin Luther King Jr., and Bill Gates, the point that striving to achieve ones goals is more important than quitting is res oundingly clear.

Model Sentences of Essay # 11

1. If the forerunners of all of these concepts and inventions had given up at the first sign of failure then we would be living in a very different world today.

2. Edison failed thousands of times before he finally progressed beyond failure and invented a working light bulb.

3. Progress in the desegregation movement in America was slow moving if not completely sedentary during the time of the great Rev. Martin Luther King Jr.

4. Despite great opposition from the majority white population in the South and government officials, King moved forward striving towards the equality he so desperately want for himself and African Americans in the United States.

5. Despite failing again, and again, Edison forged ahead,

becoming one of the most important inventors in history.

6. It all culminated into his moving "I have a dream speech" which is still used to inspire people around the world.

7. Bill Gates stood stuck in the same place for years until finally moving forward to invent the personal computer.

8. Progress in the desegregation movement in America was slow moving if not completely sedentary during the time of the great Rev. Martin Luther King Jr.

9. It all culminated into his moving "I have a dream speech" which is still used to inspire people around the world.

 What separates ordinary people from extraordinary people and their ground breaking inventions and influence, is tenacity.

> 12. Are people more efficient when confronted with the expectations and demands of others?

In this post-modern society nobody is free from the demands or expectations of others, whether one is a toddler and expected to walk by a certain age or a father expected to provide a comfortable life for his family. People are bound by the demands and expectations of others in every culture throughout the world, however the demands set forth for an individual do not necessarily further productivity. The expectations or demands of an individual lead to increased productivity only if one aims for a desired outcome and is willing to put forth the additional effort.

Productivity differs from one individual to another and depends on the setting in which one defines productivity. High school students are the epitome of subjective productivity. The goal and expectation of students once they graduate from high school, which is well accepted in society, is to attend a college or university. Although, most students tend to graduate from local or state universities, there are only a select few who manage to get accepted to elite schools. Each student decides, consciously or subconsciously, what is important and what one wants. As a result, the studen ts themselves, in the end, are responsible for their education. So, a student must have the passion and desire to attain an elite education, and must meet and, in most cases, surpass demands and expectations.

Despite a strong desire for a specific outcome, one must be willing to set out and put forth the effort. Many people want to attend and reap the privileges of attending an elite university, however desire will only get one so far. Many people also dream of living an elegant and extravagant lifestyle, but few actually do what is necessary to attain such a dream. Desire to work through the hardships and challenges that coincide with working towards a goal is the most important characteristic one must possess.

Demands and expectations are inescapable, but the level of productivity one yields depends on the desire for a goal and willingness to work. As delved into above, a student must desire academic success and be willing to put forth the effort to attain the goal. If both are met, then comes increased productivity which, in high school, means top-notch grades and other extra-curricular activities. Although, this simplifies the requirements for increasing productivity for a student, one must keep in mind that each setting differs, but one must have the desire and willingness to work.

<u>Model Sentences of Essay # 12</u>

1. People are bound by the demands and expectations of others in every culture throughout the world, however the demands set forth for an individual does not necessarily further productivity.

2. The expectations or demands of an individual leads to increased productivity only if one aims for a desired outcome and is willing to put forth the additional effort.

3. So, a student must have the passion and desire to attain an elite education, and must meet and, in most cases, surpass demands and expectations.

4. Many people want to attend and reap the privileges of attending an elite university, however desire will only get one so far.

5. As delved into above, a student must desire academic success and be willing to put forth the effort to attain the goal.

6. Demands and expectations are inescapable, but the level of productivity one yields depends on the desire for a goal and willingness to work.

Although, this simplifies the requirements for increasing productivity for a student, one must keep in mind that each setting differs.

13. Should people quit pursuing their goals when all hope is lost?

Without passion, optimism and the willingness to beli eve in the past, many accomplishments in this world, inclu ding the light bulb, might never have come to fruition. At t he same time, many lives have been wasted chasing the rai nbow's end. Similar to what my grandmother used to say, " Everything in moderation, including moderation," it is imp ortant that decisions are formulated and followed accordin g to a delicate balance.

Tim LaHaye, in his book on personality and tempera ment, theorizes that what makes a great business owner or salesperson is an indomitable spirit. It is said that, to be an effective entrepreneur, one must devote 16 hours of his da y towards the business, with the remaining eight hours for sleeping. Many people would quit pursuing their goal if sixt een hours of their waking life is needed to accomplish it. A nd the need to persevere is not limited by any means to bu siness. Where would Helen Keller have wound up if Anne Sullivan had decided that she was a hopeless case? Knowin g if and when to give up on something can change the cou rse and tenor of one's entire life.

On the flip side, similar to my grandmother's advice, my experience working as a paralegal at a bankruptcy firm, has taught me that many people hold on too long - pursuin g a dream until it devours them not only financially, but e motionally and socially as well. Not giving up often has cos ts we are unwilling to pay. The famous dancer Teri Garr w as known for her beautiful legs, but after being diagnosed with multiple sclerosis her doctor gave her the choice to gi ve up skirts for braces and pants or give up walking. There are times in life that present itself with only the option to q uit, forcing us to grudgingly move towards a new direction.

Janice Kaihoi, nurse and mother of two, decided not t o fight when diagnosed with a rare and almost incurable fo rm of cancer. She chose to embrace the remainder of her li fe with her family and live it to the fullest rather than put h erself (and her family) through months of tension and sick ness from experimental treatments. Many people around t he world face equally difficult decisions when deciding wh ether to stay with abusive or negligent spouses in order to keep their families together. The decision to call it quits ca n be an excruciating one, but at times letting go can be the best thing for everyone involved.

Like anything else in life, it's a question of balance. So me choices are easier to make than others. Whether to con tinue casually learning guitar, for example, somehow feels l ess weighty than whether or not to pursue a career in coun seling. It is not truly (for most) a question of giving up or c ontinued pursuit, but a question of what to pursue. Perhap s giving up is just an indication that whatever was is not as important as what we sacrificed it to. If something is a real passion, the odds are it will resurface again in another way even if the first course you took didn't work out.

Model Sentences of Essay # 13

1. Without passion, optimism and the willingness to believe in the past, many accomplishments in this world, including the light bulb, might never have come to fruition.

2. Similar to what my grandmother used to say, "Everything in moderation, including moderation," it is important that decisions are formulated and followed according to a delicate balance.

3. It is said that, to be an effective entrepreneur, one must devote 16 hours of their day towards the business, with the remaining eight hours for sleeping.

4. Where would Helen Keller have wound up if Anne

Sullivan had decided that she was a hopeless case?

5. On the flip side, similar to my grandmother's advice, my experience working as a paralegal at a bankruptcy firm has taught me that many people hold on too long - pursuing a dream until it devours them not only financially, but also emotionally and socially.

6. There are times in life that present itself with only the option to quit, forcing us to grudgingly move towards a new direction.

7. She chose to embrace the remainder of her life with her family and live it to the fullest rather than put herself (and her family) through months of tension and sickness from experimental treatments.

8. Many people around the world face equally difficult decisions when deciding whether to stay with abusive or negligent spouses in order to keep their families together.

9. The decision to call it quits can be an excruciating one, but at times letting go can be the best thing for everyone involved.

10. If something is a real passion, the odds are it will resurface again in another way even if the first course you took didn't work out.

14. Where do values and beliefs held by society come from?

Established values in a society originate from many sources, such as the culture, religions, and values and beliefs that a society or country was founded upon. In any given society the values of each individual vary from person to person. But there are, of course, well-accepted values throughout any society, and these values are historically present in the popular culture of a society. Whether it's the entertainment industry or health sector, the values are ingrained in the pop-culture of a society. However, there are always outliers that attempt to promote behavior or ideals that are not consistent with the values of a society.

In a society where pop-culture is synonymous with entertainment, such as the United States, it might be difficult to recognize any form of values that Americans treasure from a superficial glimpse of America. Yet, from the archetypal stories and hearsay heard at every social venue, American values are embodied. Classic stories, such as Batman, display the timeless value very dear to Americans: good over evil. From the very beginning of the idea of America, the citizens have always believed that good should prevail in an y situation. This value is very apparent today and is display ed in every aspect of the culture, from politics to advertisin g. At social gatherings people constantly discusses the chan ges in one's family and future prospects.

Despite the conspicuous values of Americans, there a re few who exploit how fast information is disseminated a nd the shock value of such information. The popularity of such questionable and shocking trends is difficult to compr ehend. Such an example is Paris Hilton. What culture whic h strongly believes in freedom, good over evil, and charity holds such a character as Paris Hilton to her level of popul arity? The answer might not be simple, however when one examines the typical "Paris fan", it becomes simple enough . It is obvious that only a very small percentage of the roug hly 300 million Americans believe that having adult footag e publically available is a good thing. Trends and fads are n ot permanent, and it is the temporary following of the few who seem to dominate the pop-culture scene.

Values and beliefs that are held by the citizens of nati ons and the society within them are derived from a multitu de of sources. With the case of America, television progra mming and music give birth to, and are reflections of, the culture of the country. The values of a society are not alwa ys apparent at first, however if one becomes familiar with a particular culture, then the values are mostly reflected in th e pop-culture of the examined society.

Model Sentences of Essay # 14

1. Established values in a society originate from many sources, such as the culture, religions, and values and beliefs that a society or country was founded upon.

2. Whether it's the entertainment industry or health sector, the values are ingrained in the pop-culture of a society.

3. In a society where pop-culture is synonymous with entertainment, such as the United States, it might be difficult to recognize any form of values that Americans treasure from a superficial glimpse of America.

4. Classic stories, such as Batman, display the timeless value very dear to Americans: good over evil.

5. Trends and fads are not permanent, and it is the temporary following of the few who seem to dominate the pop-culture scene.

6. Values and beliefs that are held by the citizens of nations and the society within them are derived from a multitude of sources.

7. With the case of America, television programming and music give birth to, and are reflections of, the culture of the country.

8. The values of a society are not always apparent at first,

however if one becomes familiar with a particular culture, then the values are mostly reflected in the pop-culture of the examined society.

9. Despite the conspicuous values of Americans, there are few who exploit how fast information is disseminated and the shock value of such information.

10. What culture which strongly believes in freedom, good over evil, and charity holds such a character as Paris Hilton to her level of popularity?

15. Are conquered dreams and aspirations of people the definition of success?

Consider, if you will, the Roman empire. Quests to conquer the world are full of what Sheri Zampelli would term, "greatest wishes and ambitions." But that does not necessarily mean that they benefit society. It depends on who is doing the conquering. Louisa May Alcott wrote in her short story "A Modern Mephistopheles," about a man who manipulated another into financial success only to observe his moral and psychological decay. More innocent but much more personal and prevalent are parents who, pursuing their dreams and goals of having successful children, push those children into long hours of study or careers they don't enjoy. Sometimes the realization of one person's goals can cost another theirs.

Who are the people pursuing their inner desires and have bettered society? Amy Carmichael spent her life caring for orphaned and abandoned children in India during the late 1800's, saving hundreds of young girls from becoming shrine prostitutes. Bill Gates founded a computer empire that jettisoned us into the modern age. Jean Valjean, of literary and operatic fame, escaped from prison and spent the remainder of his life making a fortune and helping the poor and needy. Their goals were widely different, but they each started out to improve the lives of those around them.

Perhaps what is most concerning in modern day descriptions of success is that people try to frame it as unselfish - as something deserved. Few, if any, goals are unselfish. Even the desire to be self-sacrificing is often a selfish one, enabling us to feel a superiority towards others. Whether or not society as a whole benefits from our desires or ambition depends entirely on what we set out to accomplish, however, I would have to agree with Ms. Zampelli that the world would be better off if people felt less guilty, or at least less sorry for themselves, for doing what they want.

Model Sentences of Essay # 15

1. Quests to conquer the world are full of what Sheri Zampelli would term, "greatest wishes and ambitions."

2. Louisa May Alcott wrote in her short story "A Modern Mephistopheles," about a man who manipulated another into financial success only to observe his moral and psychological decay.

3. More innocent but much more personal and prevalent are parents who, pursuing their dreams and goals of having successful children, push those children into long hours of study or careers they don't enjoy.

4. Amy Carmichael spent her life caring for orphaned and

abandoned children in India during the late 1800's, saving hundreds of young girls from becoming shrine prostitutes.

5. Bill Gates founded a computer empire that jettisoned us into the modern age.

6. Jean Val jean, of literary and operatic fame, escaped fro m prison and spent the remainder of his life making a fort une and helping the poor and needy.

7. Even the desire to be self-sacrificing is often a selfish on e, enabling us to feel a superiority towards others.

8. Whether or not society as a whole benefits from our des ires or ambition depends entirely on what we set out to acc omplish, however, I would have to agree with Ms. Zampell i that the world would be better off if people felt less guilty , or at least less sorry for themselves, for doing what they want.

> 16. Does the media provide an accurate analysis of the events of today?

The media is often accused of sensationalism or outright bias. But in many ways, this is to be expected. A media outlet is privately run or run by the state, and in both instances, they often have their own unique perspectives of the world. They'll either tow the party line in a controlled society or provide harsh criticism of the government in a freer society. The result of this is that the media will never be totally accurate. There are many reasons why the media is often inaccurate or provides a colored version of the news.

One of the first reasons is to attract an audience. People are often attracted to shocking or explicit images and descriptions. The tendency to focus on violent or shocking stories is feeding on the natural trait of seeing less mundane things that the everyday can give us. The work of the 19th century muckrakers, whose exposes of working conditions for both adult and children led to the progressive movement was one such known instance. The people were attracted to the sights and descriptions of severed limbs and suffocating bodies. It seems horrible and in many cases they were, but they attracted readers, which led to more sales an d more money being made.

Another reason that news might be skewed in one way or another is to persuade people to support a certain political position, candidate, or party. One of the most respected newspapers in Britain is The Times. This paper has been in circulation for over a century and is celebrated for its quality journalism and style. But it has traditionally been supportive of the Conservative Party and every election, they turn on the colorful support for the party. Its main competitor, The Guardian, is also known as a quality paper and supports the Labour Party. This was a tradition that began with the first political parties, so it's expected to continue today.

One last reason that the media is inaccurate is that the media outlets are being censored by the government. It has long been observed that dictatorial regimes will stop at nothing to keep power, and that includes censoring the media. The media of the Soviet Union was heavily monitored to make sure that their newspaper reporters only wrote positive stories about the system and negative stories about their enemies, both foreign and domestic. Their main newspaper, Pravda, acted as the main organ of the ruling party, so their reporters were constantly monitored for any deviation a nd were similarly removed if exposed as such. While the pa per reported only good news near the Soviet Union's end, t he whole system was collapsing.

Those are why the media is not always accurate, altho ugh it's not always their fault. The owners hold certain poli tical views and want to express their views through their m edia outlets. There's also a need to maintain profitability, w hich is often met with sensationalized stories. But the cens oring of the media through strong-arm governments is pro bably one of the biggest reasons why media often fail to m aintain accuracy. So we should take all news stories with a healthy dose of skepticism.

Model Sentences of Essay # 16

1. The media is often accused of sensationalism or outright bias.

2. A media outlet is privately run or run by the state, and in both instances, they often have their own unique perspectives of the world.

3. They'll either tow the party line in a controlled society or provide harsh criticism of the government in a freer society.
4. There are many reasons why the media is often inaccurate or provides a colored version of the news.

5. The tendency to focus on violent or shocking stories is feeding on the natural trait of seeing less mundane things

that the everyday can give us.

6. The work of the 19th century muckrakers, whose exposes of working conditions for both adult and children led to the progressive movement was one such known instance.

7. The people were attracted to the sights and descriptions of severed limbs and suffocating bodies.

8. Another reason that news might be skewed in one way or another is to persuade people to support a certain political position, candidate, or party.

9. This paper has been in circulation for over a century and is celebrated for its quality journalism and style. But it has traditionally been supportive of the Conservative Party and every election, they turn on the colorful support for the party.

10. Its main competitor, The Guardian, is also known as a quality paper and supports the Labour Party.

11. This was a tradition that began with the first political parties, so it's expected to continue today.

12. It has long been observed that dictatorial regimes will stop at nothing to keep power, and that includes censoring the media.

13. The media of the Soviet Union was heavily monitored to make sure that their newspaper reporters only wrote positive stories about the system and negative stories about their enemies, both foreign and domestic.

14. Their main newspaper, Pravda, acted as the main organ of the ruling party, so their reporters were constantly

monitored for any deviation and were similarly removed if exposed as such.

15. While the paper reported only good news near the Soviet Union's end, the whole system was collapsing.

16. Those are why the media is not always accurate, although it's not always their fault.

17. The owners hold certain political views and want to express their views through their media outlets. There's also a need to maintain profitability, which is often met with sensationalized stories.

18. But the censoring of the media through strong-arm governments is probably one of the biggest reasons why media often fail to maintain accuracy.

19. So we should take all news stories with a healthy dose of skepticism.

> 17. Is it better to rush sometimes and take action, or is it better to take time and investigate first?

The Apollo astronauts are no doubt pioneers in mann ed space flight to the moon. At the time, they risked not o nly their lives, but also their national reputation and pride. The countless man-hours and personnel that contributed t o the new NASA space program were not in vain. The pre paration involved was titanic, not because astronauts were afraid to perish, but because the consequences of failure in reaching the goal set by the late President Kennedy were w orse: losing the "space race" to the Soviets. The amount of preparation needed for any problem or challenge is never t he same, and should never be more than required for the si tuation at hand. Learning as much as possible before actin g in most situations is not necessary, unlike the Apollo Spa ce Program, because the outcome is easily anticipated and excessive preparation is a waste of resources. Thus, people should learn as much as possible for situations that will res ult in increased benefits or failure that results in irreplaceab le losses.

Most people agree that the amount of preparation is proportional to the rate of success in any given situation.

However, the extent of taking action and preparation vary considerably, such as studying for an exam and learning to fly a plane for the first time. The amount of learning and st udying before taking action should reflect the desire for th e most favorable outcome. One may not truly learn everyt hing about flying a plane from a book, but if the amount o f preparation taken is very high then it can increase the like lihood of the desired outcome: survival. Surely one would not prepare equally as much before playing a video game a s one does for preparing for actual manned flight. Neverth eless, the individual is responsible for the amount of learni ng that should take place before taking an action.

Learning as much as possible before doing anything s eems like the best way to approach an unfamiliar situation, however it is not necessary in most situations. According t o Wang Yang-ming, from *A Source Book in Chinese Philosoph y*, there are people who prefer to learn as much as possible for a situation before putting their knowledge into practice. This is not an efficient method to approach problems or p ut certain skills into use. One may learn quite a bit of theor y from a book, but the real education comes from actually practicing a skill or carrying out an action. One may choos e to learn as much as possible to ascertain the sense and ex perience of flying on a plane, but this type of preparation i s not applicable. Also, knowing how to swim is another ex ample of how one cannot adequately prepare until one has gotten into a pool.

Learning a new skill, making a decision or solving a pr oblem all requires a certain level of preparation. The amou nt of preparation and learning should fully reflect the trans lation between learning and taking action. In this way, prec ious resources, such as time, money and possibly lives, are not squandered. One should always remember, however, t hat although one may seem more than prepared before acti ng, experience is something that can never be learned from a book. In other words, experience serves information, and one can only begin reaping the benefits of valuable inform ation through trial and error.

Model Sentences of Essay # 17

1. The preparation involved was titanic, not because astronauts were afraid to perish, but because the consequences of failure in reaching the goal set by the late President Kennedy were worse: losing the "space race" to the Soviets.

2. However, the extent of taking action and preparation vary considerably, such as studying for an exam and learning to fly a plane for the first time.

3. One may not truly learn everything about flying a plane from a book, but if the amount of preparation taken is very high then it can increase the likelihood of the desired outcome: survival.

4. Learning as much as possible before doing anything seems like the best way to approach an unfamiliar situation, however it is not necessary in most situations.

5. Surely one would not prepare equally as much before playing a video game as one does for preparing for actual manned flight.

6. The amount of preparation and learning should fully reflect the translation between learning and taking action.

7. In this way, precious resources, such as time, money and possibly lives, are not squandered.

8. In other words, experience serves information, and one can only begin reaping the benefits of valuable information through trial and error.

18. Should humor be the preferred route for approaching difficult situations and problems?

There is no doubt that problems plague humanity in every crevasse of life ranging in magnitude as diverse as people themselves. Just as so, there are also many ways to solve or alleviate life's problems. Despite the limitless entirety of potential solutions most are inappropriate and excessive. One such coping technique that can putatively be applied to difficult situations is humor. Laughter is a naturally occurring pleasant phenomenon, but the contemporary recommended usage of it could result in unwanted consequences. Although some difficulties may require additional resources in terms of problem solving, time, or other means, certain problems concerning the well-being and mental health of people should not be approached lightly. Thus, I believe that using humor is not the best way to approach difficult situations.

According to Marshall Brain, the author of *How Laughter Works*, people are actually being taught to laugh at situations and things that are not necessarily humorous to cope with difficult situations. This technique may seem like a positive method to handle stressful and unpleasant situations.

However, it can potentially cause more harm than good. If one is taught to use humor to bear a situation, this may in t urn result in a diminished value and importance placed up on said situation. Just as in Pavlov's famous conditioning p sychology experiments, where a physiological response was induced from a deliberate external stimulus over a period o f time. The same can occur when using humor in the reco mmended manner. This is, however, an extreme case of w hat could happen. Nevertheless, the conditioning of the mi nd in any case can result in unforeseen consequences. One may teach themselves to laugh at friends getting hurt, and i n the future the person may find it difficult to take other si tuations seriously, and may also in turn result in social rejec tion to some degree.

One should not attempt to ease any degree of mental anxiety or stress using one approach, no matter how mild. This would be akin to treating a cancer patient with only o ne procedure. However, I do believe that it should be use d as a supplement to a more rigorous solution or treatment . The best way to approach difficult situations is being met hodical and logical. Humor should be used to lessen the de gree of a given situation or perhaps as a closure aid when a situation has been overcome, not the first or only approac

h. In cases of chronic situations, humor should definitely b e integrated to aid in the recovery process of such situation s as depression. This is consistent with current mental heal th care recommendations from any psychologist. There is a time and place for everything, and humor is no exception . Humor should be used as a supplement in coping with a difficult situation.

Humor is an excellent tool to distract one from the pa ins of reality. It also has the amazing ability to reduce the s everity of a situation. When used in the appropriate contex ts, humor is an excellent tool. However, it should never be used as the primary method to cope with a difficult situatio n. In any case, humor may seem ideal, but too much of a g ood thing will almost always result in more maladies.

Model Sentences of Essay # 18

1. There is no doubt that problems plague humanity in every crevasse of life ranging in magnitude as diverse as people themselves.

2. One such coping technique that can putatively be applied to difficult situations is humor.

3. Although some difficulties may require additional resources in terms of problem solving, time, or other means, certain problems concerning the well-being and mental health of people should not be approached lightly.

4. If one is taught to use humor to bear a situation, this may in turn result in a diminished value and importance placed upon said situation.

5. Just as in Pavlov's famous conditioning psychology experiments, where a physiological response was induced from a deliberate external stimulus over a period of time.

6. One should not attempt to ease any degree of mental anxiety or stress using one approach, no matter how mild.

7. Humor should be used to lessen the degree of a given situation or perhaps as a closure aid when a situation has been overcome, not the first or only approach.

8. Humor should be used as a supplement in coping with a difficult situation.

9. In any case, humor may seem ideal, but too much of a good thing will almost always result in more maladies.

10. However, I do believe that it should be used as a supplement to a more rigorous solution or treatment.

> 19. Are all people dependent on a social network and family, even if they choose a life of solitude?

Hilary Clinton quoted a West African proverb that said, "It takes a village to raise a family." The idea behind this simple line is complex. It implies that children need a support system, a community or a family to thrive in life and make it to adulthood and beyond. I think everyone needs a family, network or community in life, and that this idea is reflected all around the world taking many different forms. Family, or community provide support, wisdom and guidance. The need to belong is universal.

In West Africa tribal communities live together as large units. Here family takes the form of communal establishments where everyone plays a part in raising children, and household tasks. In Africa such family is necessary, as lonely individuals, or even single units of families would be unable to complete all the tasks needed to survive in the harsh environment. The building of communal families was instrumental for the survival of various African tribal communities.

In countries where one can survive alone, like the U.S, the family remains an important aspect of society. Even with a divorce rate of 50%, Americans remain dedicated to the idea of family and community. It is now simply taking a different form. The "modern American family" is usually blended, consisting of step fathers, mothers, and step siblings. Despite marriages not surviving in the U.S., the idea of family is thriving. Nowhere is the idea that everyone needs a family or family like unit more prevalent than in the prison system. In prison, even criminals come together to form gangs, and makeshift families, so that they feel like they belong. Another example of the importance of family is reflected in suicide rates. Most people who commit suicide feel "alone" and usually don't feel as if they belong anywhere.

For humans, the need for contact and connection is important. People in all countries, and situations seek out companionship. Having a family has become a basic human need, like shelter or food.

Model Sentences of Essay # 19

1. It implies that children need a support system, a community or a family to thrive in life and make it to adulthood and beyond.

2. Here family takes the form of communal establishments where everyone plays a part in raising children, and household tasks.

3. Even with a divorce rate of 50%, Americans remain dedicated to the idea of family and community.

4. The "modern American family" is usually blended, consisting of step fathers, mothers, and step siblings.

5. In prison, even criminals come together to form gangs, and makeshift families, so that they feel like they belong.

6. People in all countries, and situations seek out companionship.

7. Having a family has become a basic human need, like shelter or food.

> 20. Do you agree that our society has become too negative and less sensitive?

Looking at the condition of modern society begs the question: have we become overly cynical and desensitized? Ironically, we must also ask if there is hope to end this culture of cynicism. It is clear that it is time for a change, but it will be difficult because cynicism is so deeply entrenched in our perceptions of the world. According to Positive Psychologist Mihaly Csikszentmihalyi, much of modern "human development", including humanities, politics, science and technology has ignored basic human strengths and virtues that are worth cultivating. The leadership in both academia and "the real world" has been taken over by those who have promoted this culture of self-congratulatory cynicism. This trend has overflowed from the "ivory tower" of the elite into everyday lives of everyday people.

According to a recent political survey in the United States, the common citizen believes that the next ten years will not be as good as the last. People no longer seem to see the joy in the little things that make life worth living. This trend seems especially apparent in young people who are being force-fed a commercialized vision of "the good life" an d at the same moment, are bombarded with violence, melo dramatic babble, and expansive wealth. These extremes de sensitize the viewer to such an extent that many now are u nable to value basic human experiences.

This culture of cynicism stems from the basic fact tha t people have lost faith in "progress." The advances in scie nce, technology, art and philosophy, which are meant to br ing people forward, has not prevented world wars, depressi on, poverty and sickness. If anything, this "progress" has p ulled us further away from what is truly important, people. In order to turn our society around and bring us back to " our roots" if you will, it is necessary to change our percepti on of "progress."

Progress must start positive cultural values. Each indi vidual must recognize the importance of long-term happin ess; that what pleases us in the moment won't necessarily make us happy later in life, and we must recognize those th at rejoice in the simple fact of being human. Once this new definition of progress is adopted and joined with "tradition al" progress, the general perception of the future will chan ge. People will no longer believe that we are headed down a doomed path. We will naturally make choices that take in to account the well-being of everyone and this culture of c ynicism will develop into a culture of optimism.

Model Sentences of Essay # 20

1. Looking at the condition of modern society begs the question: have we become overly cynical and desensitized?

2. According to Positive Psychologist Mihaly Csikszentmihalyi, much of modern "human development," including humanities, politics, science and technology has ignored basic human strengths and virtues that are worth cultivating.

3. The leadership in both academia and "the real world" has been taken over by those who have promoted this culture of self-congratulatory cynicism.

4. This trend seems especially apparent in young people who are being force-fed a commercialized vision of "the good life" and at the same moment, are bombarded with violence, melodramatic babble, and expansive wealth.

5. These extremes desensitize the viewer to such an extent that many now are unable to value basic human experiences.

6. The advances in science, technology, art and philosophy, which are meant to bring people forward, have not prevented world wars, depression, poverty and sickness.

7. In order to turn our society around and bring us back to "our roots" if you will, it is necessary to change our perception of "progress."

> 21. Do you believe art and creativity should always be associated with anguish, suffering, and pain?

Nowadays, creativity manifests itself in seemingly end less forms throughout all fields of study. Every field from complex quantum mechanics to modern dance, creative in dividuals have undertaken novel, often unsuccessful, paths in their careers. Without these pioneering people, fields in art and science would lay stagnant. Although great strides have been made in art and science, the 'artists' have been t he ones that have endured criticism, from others, and see mingly worse, themselves. Artists are constantly pursuing p erfection, and it seems that the best nurturers for their crea tivity are themselves. Although tending to creativity and str iving for perfection are important, they can also lead to des tructive behaviors.

Many well-known and unfamiliar artists have succum bed to misery in one form or another. Whether suffering u nfolds in episodes of depression or chemical dependency, t he reason is almost always related to creative roadblocks. F ortunately, most roadblocks are short-lived and rarely deve lop into serious afflictions. However, in some cases, misery is a common component among artists before they ever st art creating artistic works. Art may become one's escape fr om reality or melancholy that may have served as motivati on. In the case of J. K. Rowling, she endured years of hard ship and secretly wrote about a young boy who would bec ome a famous wizard to escape her reality. Many famous a rtists throughout time have become famous because of the ir works, rather than their episodes of grief.

In conclusion, the pattern of grief about one's work s eems to be more prevalent these days. This awareness is pe rhaps due to advancements in communication and the sub sequent "shrinking" of the world. Artistry, as a result, has been labeled a field with inescapable heartache. There are t housands of artists throughout the world, and the associati on of anguish with creativity is the consequence of a minut e group of audacious artists. In every society, there are few people who crave attention in any form, positive or negativ e. Perhaps if these few people cannot be successful in their endeavors in creativity, they dwell in the spotlight of torme nt.

Like many professions, artists experience anguish. Th e experiences of artists in grief are almost always short-live d. Anguish is not a permanent disposition, but serves as a c reative hurdle, one that must be overcome in order to flour

ish. The stereotype that artists will ultimately be miserable i
s false; it is thought so by the few ill-natured people that de
pict this grim lifestyle. It is the responsibility of art enthusi
asts to realize that anguish is not exclusive to artists.

Model Sentences of Essay # 21

1. Nowadays, creativity manifests itself in seemingly endless forms throughout all fields of study.

2. Every field from complex quantum mechanics to modern dance, creative individuals have undertaken novel, often unsuccessful, paths in their careers

3. Artists are constantly pursuing perfection, and it seems that the best nurturers for their creativity are themselves.

4. Whether suffering unfolds in episodes of depression or chemical dependency, the reason is almost always related to creative roadblocks.

5. Art may become one's escape from reality or melancholy that may have served as motivation.

6. Artistry, as a result, has been labeled a field with inescapable heartache.

7. Perhaps if these few people cannot be successful in their endeavors in creativity, they dwell in the spotlight of torment.

8. Anguish is not a permanent disposition, but serves as a creative hurdle, one that must be overcome in order to flourish.

9. There are thousands of artists throughout the world, and the association of anguish with creativity is the consequence of a minute group of audacious artists.

10. Although tending to creativity and striving for perfection are important, they can also lead to destructive behaviors.

> 22. Is life predetermined or do people have the ability to pave their own paths in life?

The search for answers to all life's mysteries is an inherent part of the human psyche. Throughout history, human beings have invented numerous theories to explain paranormal and metaphysical phenomenon. Before important discoveries, such as microscopic organisms and their role in diseases, many believed that certain malicious behaviors caused such disease, and a "higher power" was ultimately responsible for their fate. The notion that our lives are premeditated, whether by a higher being or not, is nonsense.

In W. W. Jacob's *The Monkey's Paw*, a supposed enchanted talisman held the power to grant three wishes to three men. Each wish would be granted, however, the wish would not be granted in a fairy-tale manner, but in a seemingly coincidental way. In the story, the father wished for a sum of money and he was granted his wish, but was granted it in an unforeseen trade for his son's life. In a scene prior to the son's death and payment of the money, the family is gathered and the father wishes for a sum of money. Afterwards, the son says, "Well, I don't see the money, and I bet I never shall." Although this story shows that wishing is magi cal and coincidental, the son himself is most likely responsible for the outcome. Perhaps feeling that the family greatly desired the money, the son took matters into his own hands.

The idea that each of our lives is predetermined is not logical. People make hundreds, if not thousands, of decisions a day. The sheer complexity of human beings' thought processes consequently results in inconsistent decision-making. Add countless daily influences to this already dynamic high functioning being, and the notion of destiny is absurd. Coincidences and events that one believes lead to destiny are merely a result of including people in one's life; whether they share similar beliefs or are integral in lifestyle or career.

Destiny is a human invention designed to explain seemingly impossible coincidences and fantastic events. Though destiny may appear to be paranormal or the responsibility of a higher power, it is perhaps an unborn precursor to a novel science in sociology or other related field. The choices one makes can directly or indirectly affect another individual, however, the magnitude of the affect depends on the choice itself. Therefore, one's 'destiny' is not predetermined; rather it is the responsibility of each individual to sculpt his or her own life.

Model Sentences of Essay # 22

1. The search for answers to all life's mysteries is an inherent part of the human psyche.

2. Throughout history, human beings have invented numerous theories to explain paranormal and metaphysical phenomenon.

3. Before important discoveries, such as microscopic organisms and their role in diseases, many believed that certain malicious behaviors caused such disease, and a "higher power" was ultimately responsible for their fate.

4. In the story, the father wished for a sum of money and he was granted his wish, but was granted it in an unforeseen trade for his son's life.

5. Perhaps feeling that the family greatly desired the money, the son took matters into his own hands.

6. The sheer complexity of human beings' thought processes consequently results in inconsistent decision-making.

7. Add countless daily influences to this already dynamic high functioning being, and the notion of destiny is absurd.

> 23. Should the definition of courage be restricted to people who risk their own well-being for the good of others or should it also be expanded to people who uphold values?

Courageous deeds fit into a variety of categories. Though acts of self-sacrifice for the sake of others are without a doubt courageous, we need not use such conservative nomenclature in discussing human behavior. One can argue semantics regarding the differences in connotation among words such as "adventuresome" and "courageous," but the decision to allow the word courage to have a broader range of meaning remains valid, and in some ways any attempt to do otherwise merely belittles the actions of courageous men and women.

One can see examples of courage in many endeavors other than unselfish acts of heroism. Was Rosa Parks not courageous in her unwillingness to be deemed a second-class citizen and sit at the back of the bus in Montgomery, Alabama? Were the men and women killed in Tiananmen Square while standing up to the PRC government not courageous? Equating these heroic actions with "....differ[ing] from the mainstream in one's preferences in fashion or music

" is simply insulting. Wearing leopard-print shoes is not co urageous; standing up to a force greater than you in the na me of justice is the definition of courage.

Cases need not be so extreme to warrant the usage of the word courageous. It takes true courage to do many dee ds not nearly as lofty as those of Rosa Parks and others. Be ing true to oneself about what one really wants in life is an act of incredible courage. A genuine, unfeigned decision ta kes tremendous honesty and courage to make: honesty to be willing to say what you want, and courage to do so. Eve n things like bungee jumping and skydiving require a certai n degree of courage. Again, there are indeed slight differen ces between words like "courage" and "daring", but they a re futile and ultimately meaningless distinctions in regards t o a discussion of people's actions.

Attempting to make certain acts seem more worthy th an others by calling them courageous is not of value. In fac t, to call these actions anything less than courageous is to d isparage the efforts of men and women of the past and pre sent who deserve a greater level of respect.

Model Sentences of Essay # 23

1. One can argue semantics regarding the differences in connotation among words such as "adventuresome" and

"courageous," but the decision to allow the word courage to have a broader range of meaning remains valid, and in some ways any attempt to do otherwise merely belittles the actions of courageous men and women.

2. Equating these heroic actions with "....differ[ing] from the mainstream in one's preferences in fashion or music" is simply insulting.

3. Wearing leopard-print shoes is not courageous; standing up to a force greater than you in the name of justice is the definition of courage.

4. Cases need not be so extreme to warrant the usage of the word courageous.

5. A genuine, unfeigned decision takes tremendous honesty and courage to make: honesty to be willing to say what you want, and courage to do so.

6. Again, there are indeed slight differences between words like "courage" and "daring", but they are futile and ultimately meaningless distinctions in regards to a discussion of people's actions.

7. In fact, to call these actions anything less than courageous is to disparage the efforts of men and women of the past and present who deserve a greater level of respect.

24. Is it feasible for a society to simultaneously offer perfect equality and perfect freedom?

When Thomas Jefferson wrote into the constitution " ...all men are created equal", he did not intend to sound off as though he believed that all men have identical abilities, f laws, ambitions, and dreams. He meant that we are all equa l in the eyes of God and the law. We can aspire to that kin d of equality, but aspiring to even approach equality in oth er ways necessarily compromises the freedom of individual s.

Helping people with limited opportunities or abilities to have decent lives requires money. This money must co me from people who have more; if the government does n ot have the money to help the poor, they will continue to s uffer. If we believe that citizens should have the basics of li fe, such as food, shelter, and healthcare, thus making them to a degree more equal with more prosperous people, one of the freedoms of the rich, the freedom to do whatever th ey want with their money, must be compromised. We end up with neither perfect equality nor perfect freedom, but s omeplace in between, where everyone has something.

Anatole France wrote sarcastically, "The law, in its ma

jestic equality, forbids the rich as well as the poor to beg in the streets, steal bread, or sleep under a bridge." We are, in principle if not fully in reality, both free and equal under th e law. In the real world, however, some people, through ed ucation, innate ability, family connections, or money, have far more opportunities than others; they eat better, travel more freely, enjoy life more, and live longer. That's fine; tr ue communism leads only to misery, because human natur e demands more for the self and less for strangers. But we can at least attempt to give the poorest among us a meal, a bed, and a chance.

In the end, we can't be both truly free and truly equal. There is a balance that must be held, with perfect equality and perfect freedom being constantly undergoing a negotia tion. The fact is that these two wonderful ideals are always, to a degree, at war, and the only way to lasting justice lies i n reaching a peace treaty between the two. We must respec t both.

Model Sentences of Essay # 24

1. When Thomas Jefferson wrote into the constitution "...all men are created equal", he did not intend to sound off as though he believed that all men have identical abilities, flaws, ambitions, and dreams.

2. We can aspire to that kind of equality, but aspiring to even approach equality in other ways necessarily compromises the freedom of individuals.

3. Anatole France wrote sarcastically, "The law, in its majestic equality, forbids the rich as well as the poor to beg in the streets, steal bread, or sleep under a bridge."

4. We are, in principle if not fully in reality, both free and equal under the law.

5. In the real world, however, some people, through education, innate ability, family connections, or money, have far more opportunities than others; they eat better, travel more freely, enjoy life more, and live longer.

6. There is a balance that must be held, with perfect equality and perfect freedom being constantly undergoing a negotiation.

7. The fact is that these two wonderful ideals are always, to a degree, at war, and the only way to lasting justice lies in reaching a peace treaty between the two.

25. Are there social situations when impolite behavior is necessary?

Good manners have virtually disappeared from our self-centered world. People butt into line at the supermarket, guests on political news shows shout at each other, fist fights break out in the Korean National Assembly. Many believe that it's essential to be rude or aggressive to change the world for the better. Of course, each person thinks that his version of "better" is the only one that counts, and that leads to anger on all sides. Actually, though, it is better to be as polite as possible in all circumstances, even when that is not the same as never offending anyone.

The twentieth century's greatest moral leaders, the people who truly improved the world, conducted themselves with great dignity and politeness. Mahatma Gandhi, Nelson Mandela, and Martin Luther King, Jr. achieved great things by loving their enemies while calmly and politely demonstrating against their moral failures. The great religious sages throughout the centuries, such as Jesus and Buddha, did not have to insult people or shout at them to get their points across. All of these people can only be called impolite if we define that word as telling the truth to those who don't

want to hear it. But the truth can be told with dignity, com
passion, and manners.

In everyday life, we all sometimes must do things that
seem rude. We may have to sever relations with a romantic
partner, fire an unsatisfactory employee, or confront some
one who's harming someone else. But all of these can be d
one with respect for the other person's point of view; any
action can be done rudely or kindly, and there's no reason
not to choose kindness. Although the person we confront
will be hurt or angry, those feelings are tempered, in the lo
ng run, by the memory of how the unpleasant event was h
andled.

In the final analysis, being as polite as possible is the k
ey guideline. It's impossible to avoid ever raising one's voic
e or upsetting someone; sometimes truths must be told, ev
en when it hurts. But anything that must be done can be d
one with kindness. Doing so can only make a bad situation
better for everyone concerned and add a tiny bit to the har
mony of our world.

Model Sentences of Essay # 25

1. Good manners have virtually disappeared from our self-
centered world.

2. People butt into line at the supermarket, guests on

political news shows shout at each other, fist fights break out in the Korean National Assembly.

3. Actually, though, it is better to be as polite as possible in all circumstances, even when that is not the same as never offending anyone.

4. The twentieth century's greatest moral leaders, the people who truly improved the world, conducted themselves with great dignity and politeness.

5. Mahatma Gandhi, Nelson Mandela, and Martin Luther King, Jr. achieved great things by loving their enemies while calmly and politely demonstrating against moral failures.

6. The great religious sages throughout the centuries, such as Jesus and Buddha, did not have to insult people or shout at them to get their points across.

7. In everyday life, we all sometimes must do things that seem rude. We may have to sever relations with a romantic partner, fire an unsatisfactory employee, or confront someone who's harming someone else.

26. Does ethical behavior impede the pursuit of success?

"Nice guys finish last," the American baseball manager Leo Durocher famously said, articulating the common belief that it takes unethical behavior—lying, bending the rules, cheating—to win. Although he was talking about a baseball pennant race, people in many walks of life have subscribed to, and secretly followed, his prescription for winning. In the end, though, what *is* success? Becoming rich and famous may or may not require dishonest behavior, but a moral code is not a hindrance to true success, it's an absolute necessity.

First we should examine whether unethical conduct leads to success. For everyone who has achieved their goals through trickery, another has done so by maintaining his moral code. Being honest and reliable leads to trust from others, and a good reputation is a powerful tool to what the world calls "success."

While it's true that many devious people have risen to the heights of society, often they come crashing to the ground. For example, the most famous American baseball players of their era, Mark McGwire, Barry Bonds, and Roger

Clemens, have been revealed as steroid users and liars. They have their millions of dollars, but have lost the respect (and sometimes adulation) of a world of baseball fans. Ken Lay of Enron Corporation died waiting to be imprisoned; Bernie Madoff, who stole hundreds of billions of dollars of his clients' money, will spend the rest of his life in jail. Was it worth it?

What is success, anyway? That, as Hamlet said, is the question. Is it being famous, or rich, or powerful? Those things certainly seem like success to many people. Although people say that money can't buy happiness, it can certainly rent it. It would be more fun to spend the weekend lying on the beach in Hawaii or skiing in the French Alps than trudging from home to work and back again in midwinter. But true success is not about money, or fame, or even happiness. Success is being able to sleep at night and look yourself in the eye in your mirror every morning. It's knowing that you have helped others, that the world is a tiny bit better because you're in it.

Every major religion in the world shares the same message: we are on earth to help each other. Money is nice, but plays a limited factor in bringing about true happiness. Fame is fine, but it fades. Power means always looking over your shoulder to see who wants to take it away. You are no t a success unless you have the respect of those around yo u and, more importantly, of yourself. Success is a clear con science, a peaceful mind, and someone to love. True succe ss is impossible without morality.

Model Sentences of Essay # 26

1. "Nice guys finish last," the American baseball manager Leo Durocher famously said, articulating the common belief that it takes unethical behavior—lying, bending the rules, cheating—to win.

2. Although he was talking about a baseball pennant race, people in many walks of life have subscribed to, and secretly followed, his prescription for winning.

3. Becoming rich and famous may or may not require dishonest behavior, but a moral code is not a hindrance to true success, it's an absolute necessity.

4. Being honest and reliable leads to trust from others, and a good reputation is a powerful tool to what the world calls "success."

5. For example, the most famous American baseball players of their era, Mark McGwire, Barry Bonds, and Roger Clemens, have been revealed as steroid users and liars.

6. Although people say that money can't buy happiness, it can certainly rent it.

7. It would be more fun to spend the weekend lying on the beach in Hawaii or skiing in the French Alps than trudging from home to work and back again in midwinter.

8. Money is nice, but plays a limited factor in bringing about true happiness.

9. You are not a success unless you have the respect of those around you and, more importantly, of yourself.

10. Success is being able to sleep at night and look yourself in the eye in your mirror every morning.

27. What is more reflective of personal character: actions or words?

Do actions or words reveal a person's true attitudes? I 'd say it depends. First, everyone perceives the same perso n differently. Second, people's attitude changes overtime. Even though there can be a consistent pattern in one's beh avior, it is extremely difficult to predict it accurately becaus e everyone thinks and acts differently. Eastern and western philosophies discuss similar topics in their texts, as well as contemporary psychologists in the 20th and 21st century.

Many philosophers and scientists have said that one's perspective plays an important role in an observation. For example, Buddha once said, "Those whose mind is rich al ways finds others rich." Here, he meant that one's view ca n be skewed depending on the person's state of mind. Hun dreds of years later in Europe, David Hume said, "Human s can only perceive what they can pick up from their sense s." Such Hume's philosophy can be well explained by our modern day medical science.

According to Ramachandran, a contemporary neurolo gist, human brains contain mirror neurons which help peo ple understand and learn from others through imitation. In other words, if people can relate a behavior that they see to their past experience, they can judge and understand other s better. However, if they can't, they might not readily acce pt or comprehend the person's behavior. Since everyone p erceives others' behaviors differently (or see things from th eir own perspectives), one's true intentions can be read diff erently.

Thirdly, most human thoughts change naturally accor ding to time and location. This means people's thoughts an d emotions may change from time to time, even if they are read correctly. For example, a French philosopher, Jean Pa ul Sartre's philosophy evolved as he aged. As a young write r, he believed human behavior could be read quite accurate ly as they think and behave in a pattern. However, by the ti me he died, he said, "We can only perceive a fragment of what one thinks." An ancient Chinese philosopher, Lao Ts u used to describe a human mind as "the myriad creatures, " and I think he explained this complexity very well.

A human mind is just as complicated as our neural str uctures of the brain. Millions of neurons are inter-connecte d and they function instantaneously. If one can catch that a nd distinguish it as "one thought," only then, can he argue that a man's intention or behavior can be read fairly accura tely.

Model Sentences of Essay # 27

1. Even though there can be a consistent pattern in one's behavior, it is extremely difficult to predict it accurately because everyone thinks and acts differently.

2. According to Ramachandran, a contemporary neurologist, human brains contain mirror neurons that help people understand and learn from others through imitation.

3. Since everyone perceives others' behaviors differently (or from their own perspectives), one's true intentions can be read differently.

4. As a young writer, he believed human behavior could be read quite accurately as they think and behave in a pattern.

5. An ancient Chinese philosopher, Lao Tsu used to describe a human mind as "the myriad creatures," and I think he explained this complexity very well.

6. A human mind is just as complicated as our neural structures of the brain.

7. Millions of neurons are inter-connected and they function instantaneously.

28. Are lives improved when changes are made?

Change has an effect on everybody that either has a h and in it or is somehow affected by it tangentially. It can b e a big help or a major hindrance depending on who you a sk. The type of change that is made will either be minor, af fecting a single person, or it could be large, affecting the w hole society. Here are some major changes that have prove n to be positive to society.

The world once believed in things that we find either horrifying of simply silly. And it was these beliefs that led t o the practices of medicine for a while. But one of the first major changes came with the proposal of germ theory. Wit h the invention of microscopes and the first abilities to see organisms that were too small for the naked eye, a better u nderstanding of disease was obtained. Edward Jenner was one of the first to use the finding of these discoveries to pr oduce vaccines against feared diseases like smallpox. Other breakthroughs in medicine followed as scientists continued using microscopes and other instruments to explore the in ner working of the human body. The switch from superstit ion to science was a major change that benefitted everybod y.

The products that we buy were once made by hand b y a single person. Then they became made on assembly lin es. This improved lives by being able to increase the numb er of products available and thus the amount of wealth gre w as they became more abundant and cheaper. But the wo rkers weren't helped out until they were guaranteed safe w orking conditions. But the biggest change was automation, when robots replaced human laborers, this was painful at fi rst, but then people were able to adjust to the new hi-tech world, but people soon embraced it and now the most eco nomically strong countries are the most tech savvy. From one person, to many people, to no people, production imp rovements have improved lives in many ways.

Perhaps lives have improved the most when the way people were governed changed from unaccountable monar ch to more accountable representatives. The hereditary mo narchs of the old world viewed themselves as divinely app ointed and didn't care for what the people thought about t hem. This upset the people and led to revolutions. After a period of chaos, enlightened thinkers were able to set of g overnments made of people chosen by people. These gove rnments could be replaced when they weren't working out, something that couldn't happen with a dictatorial king. Thi s change was probably the biggest in history.

People today are healthier, freer, and richer thanks to the changes of the past. It remains to be seen how people's lives will be improved by the future's changes.

Model Sentences of Essay # 28

1. Change has an effect on everybody that either has a hand in it or is somehow affected by it tangentially.

2. It can be a big help or a major hindrance depending on who you ask.

3. The type of change that is made will either be minor, affecting a single person, or it could be large, affecting the whole society.

4. The world once believed in things that we find either horrifying of simply silly.

5. With the invention of microscopes and the first abilities to see organisms that were too small for the naked eye, a better understanding of disease was obtained.

6. Edward Jenner was one of the first to use the finding of these discoveries to produce vaccines against feared diseases like smallpox.

7. Other breakthroughs in medicine followed as scientists continued using microscopes and other instruments to explore the inner working of the human body.

8. The switch from superstition to science was a major change that benefitted everybody.

9. But the workers weren't helped out until they were guaranteed safe working conditions.

10. From one person, to many people, to no people, production improvements have improved lives in many ways.

11. Perhaps lives have improved the most when the way people were governed changed from unaccountable monarch to more accountable representatives.

12. The hereditary monarchs of the old world viewed themselves as divinely appointed and didn't care for what the people thought about them.

13. After a period of chaos, enlightened thinkers were able to set of governments made of people chosen by people.

14. These governments could be replaced when they weren't working out, something that couldn't happen with a dictatorial king.

15. People today are healthier, freer, and richer thanks to the changes of the past.

16. It remains to be seen how people's lives will be improved by the future's changes.

29. What important qualities are shared by famous or successful people?

Abraham Lincoln and Charles Darwin each did something that perhaps no other person could have done. Lincoln, through his political ability and force of will, kept the United States a unified country and ended 250 years of slavery in America. Darwin went on a five-year voyage and worked for over 20 years to formulate his theory of evolution, which overturned pre-nineteenth century superstition. What Lincoln and Darwin had in common was keen intelligence and fierce will.

Lincoln was a little-known backwoods politician when he ran for president, and then, seemingly, was unexpectedly elected president. His ambition and political skill helped vault him over many more famous candidates. Once he was president, he was resolute in not allowing the Southern states leave the Union. He did not allow the Northern states to stop fighting. It was only his determination that saved the country; perhaps no one else could have done it. He used his intelligence to see the war to its conclusion, speaking eloquently of the cause and, when the time was right, freeing the slaves. Extraordinary times demand extraordinar y men. Lincoln came from the frontier at the exact momen t his nation needed him.

Darwin's voyage on *HMS Beagle* took him from Engla nd to South America, Africa, and Australia. During those fi ve years, he collected fossils and studied living birds, turtle s, and other animals. Drawing especially from his observati ons in the Galapagos Islands off South America, he began to formulate his theory of evolution. His will led him to de vote nearly thirty years of his life to the voyage and to for mulating his ideas, and to dare to publish a theory that ove rturned thousands of years of spiritual belief and outraged religious people worldwide. His intelligence led him to see connections where no one before him had. Darwin is the most important figure in changing our world view from su perstition to science.

Both men, Abraham Lincoln and Charles Darwin, sha red the quality of having a strong sense of tenacity and bra very. With Darwin, it was his courage to challenge the hith erto established doctrine of creationism. Abraham Lincoln, similarly, had the courage to finally put to question the issu e of slavery and solve it once and for all.

Model Sentences of Essay # 29

1. Lincoln, through his political ability and force of will, kept the United States a unified country and ended 250 years of slavery in America.

2. Darwin went on a five-year voyage and worked for over 20 years to formulate his theory of evolution, which overturned pre-nineteenth century superstition.

3. Lincoln was a little-known backwoods politician when he ran for president, and then, seemingly, was unexpectedly elected president.

4. He used his intelligence to see the war to its conclusion, speaking eloquently of the cause and, when the time was right, freeing the slaves.

5. Drawing especially from his observations in the Galapagos Islands off South America, he began to formulate his theory of evolution.

6. His will led him to devote nearly thirty years of his life to the voyage and to formulating his ideas, and to dare to publish a theory that overturned thousands of years of spiritual belief and outraged religious people worldwide

7. With Darwin, it was his courage to challenge the hitherto established doctrine of creationism.

> 30. What plays a larger role for achieving success: effort or good fortune?

Effort and luck are intertwined in life. They are linked together like a DNA string; effort and luck determine a person's future. Indeed, success in life is earned and a matter of luck.

Obviously, success is an amalgamation of factors. People are more likely to achieve and be successful if they work hard and set goals. The foundation of education is constructed of discipline, diligence and a look toward the future and success. Still, education and all that it entails is not a guaranteed recipe for success. Dedication, personal character and effort may not be enough.

The problem involves the luck of the draw. Life to a great extent is like a poker game and success may depend on the cards dealt to you. Let's look at an example, albeit an extreme one. Clearly, if a child is born in the poorest regions of Africa, or any other third-world country, he will not likely have the same opportunities as young people do in Western nations. In fact, instead of encountering opportunities, people in such forlorn countries often are confronted with misery and devastation. Success, along with education, may be just a concept or dream to them. To state that such people can succeed simply based on the ability to work hard and earn their way is preposterous. On the other hand, to emphasize that luck simply causes the success of a person is just as wrongheaded and perhaps insulting. "I'd never yell 'Good luck!' at anybody," said Holden Caulfield, the protagonist in J.D. Salinger's *The Catcher in the Rye*. "It sounds terrible, when you think about it."

Still another example of luck's power relates to being born into royalty. Does anyone really think that the obvious success of Prince William is much more than luck? From conception, luck has accompanied the presumptive future king of England. Yes, he has studied hard and gone to the best schools. And, his strength of character may well contribute to being an accomplished king one day. But, his success is interwoven with luck.

Having said that, hard work and all those other traits founded in education can lead to success. Again, those qualities are not a guarantee of achievement. However, people who strive and earn their way can be ready for the possibility of success, when it comes through opportunities. Seneca, a Roman philosopher, said in the mid-1st Century AD, "Luck is what happens when preparation meets opportunity.

"

So, what does it take to be prepared for opportunity? No matter where they are born or live, people must learn and embrace knowledge, whether through formal education or personal experience. People must strive and earn their way in life. Then they will be ready to take advantage of luck, which, perhaps, could come in ordinary forms such as business, professional or educational opportunities. Many successful people will tell you that their achievements in life were due at least in part to luck. They were in the right place at the right time.

Therefore, success in life is earned and a matter of luck. Thomas Jefferson, the third U.S. president, addressed the issue. He said, "I'm a great believer in luck, and I find the harder I work, the more I have of it."

Model Sentences of Essay # 32

1. They are linked together like a DNA string; effort and luck determine a person's future.

2. Obviously, success is an amalgamation of factors.

3. The foundation of education is constructed of discipline, diligence and a look toward the future and success.

4. Life to a great extent is like a poker game and success may depend on the cards dealt to you.

5. Clearly, if a child is born in the poorest regions of Africa , or any other third-world country, he will not likely have t he same opportunities as young people do in Western nati ons.

6. In fact, instead of encountering opportunities, people in such forlorn countries often are confronted with misery an d devastation.

7. On the other hand, to emphasize that luck simply causes the success of a person is just as wrongheaded and perhaps insulting.

8. From conception, luck has accompanied the presumptiv e future king of England.

9. Then they will be ready to take advantage of luck, which , perhaps, could come in ordinary forms such as business, professional or educational opportunities.

Made in the USA
Middletown, DE
18 February 2016